© Copyright 2022 - All rights reserved.

The content contained within this book may not be reproduced, duplicated or transmitted without direct written permission from the author or the publisher.
Under no circumstances will any blame or legal responsibility be held against the publisher, or author, for any damages, reparation, or monetary loss due to the information contained within this book, either directly or indirectly.

Legal Notice:
This book is copyright protected. It is only for personal use. You cannot amend, distribute, sell, use, quote or paraphrase any part, or the content within this book, without the consent of the author or publisher.

Author: Jed Dolton
Publisher: Daoudi Publishing
ISBN: 978-1-960809-10-0

TABLE OF CONTENT

B	1 - 6
D	7 - 12
P	13 - 18
Q	19 - 24
U	25 - 30
V	31 - 36
W	37 - 42
F	43 - 48
T	49 - 54
M	55 - 60
N	61 - 66
X	67 - 72
Y	73 - 78
Z	79 - 84
B R	85 - 90
P L	91 - 96
B L	97 - 102
D R	103 - 108
P H	109 - 114
Q U	115 - 120
S P	121 - 126
S C	127 - 132
S H	133 - 138
O I	139 - 144
O E	145 - 150
E I	151 - 156
E A	157 - 162
A U	163 - 168
A W	169 - 174
E W	175 - 180

INTRODUCTION

This book is a valuable tool for young readers, specifically designed for kindergarten students who are learning to read. It focuses on the important skill of decoding words and aims to help struggling readers improve their reading abilities at the word level. The book consists of 30 reading passages, each with comprehension questions to ensure that students understand what they have read.

The passages in the book use only decodable words, which means that they are made up of letters and letter combinations that students have already learned. This approach enables children to read independently and helps them gain confidence in their reading abilities.

The book follows a structured approach, teaching children the sounds that letters make (phonemes) in a specific order. It starts with the most commonly used phonemes and progresses to more complex ones. The activities included in each passage are designed to reinforce phonemic awareness and promote skill development, such as identifying sounds, tracing letters, filling in missing letters, and more.

Whether your child is a reluctant reader or struggling with reading, this book is a valuable resource for parents and teachers. It is convenient, easy to use, and provides an effective way to help young readers build a solid foundation in reading. With the help of this book, your child will be on their way to becoming a confident and proficient reader in no time.

THIS BOOK BELONG TO

_____

I CAN READ

Read the story, and identify and underline all the - b - words.

Berry Baking Adventure

Benny Bear was a big, brown bear who loved to play with his friends. He bounced a ball and blew bubbles. One day, he went for a walk in the woods and saw a butterfly. He chased it and bumped into a beehive. The bees buzzed and Benny ran, but he fell into a bush. He brushed off the bugs and found some berries. He picked them and brought them to his buddies. They baked a yummy pie and ate it together. Benny smiled, feeling blessed.

read and write

Write all the "b" words you can see in the story			

I CAN READ

Read the sentences and answers the questions: Put a check mark

Billy the bunny was bored

Jack bought butter and flour

He mixed and baked them

Questions

1. Who was feeling bored?   the bunny billy ☐   dog ☐
2. What did Jack buy?   car ☐   butter and flour ☐

Write the correct word beside each scrambled word.

bta _____	bgi _____	bsu _____
bga _____	bxo _____	biek _____
bde _____	byo _____	bidr _____

Make sentences

Bat _____
_____
_____

Bag _____
_____
_____

Rules
TRACE AND COLOR

Trace it:

B B B B

b b b b

box   box   box

Colour it:

I CAN WRITE

Color Me!

bird

Circle the - b - words

fear	anglo	blue
ball	gear	book
near	bone	angas

Trace the words

bike bike
boy boy
bell bell

Fill in the missing letters

be ____   bi ____
bu ____   bo ____
ba ____   be ____

Read and Trace the sentence.

I Have a Bag
i have a bag

READ AGAIN

Read the story, and answer each question. highlight the answers in the story.

Berry Baking Adventure

Benny Bear was a big, brown bear who loved to play with his friends. He bounced a ball and blew bubbles. One day, he went for a walk in the woods and saw a butterfly. He chased it and bumped into a beehive. The bees buzzed and Benny ran, but he fell into a bush. He brushed off the bugs and found some berries. He picked them and brought them to his buddies. They baked a yummy pie and ate it together. Benny smiled, feeling blessed.

Answer Each Question.

1 - What kind of animal was Benny?

_____

2 - What did Benny do for fun with his friends?

_____

3 - What did Benny see when he went for a walk in the woods?

_____

COLOR ME

Read and color the Letter

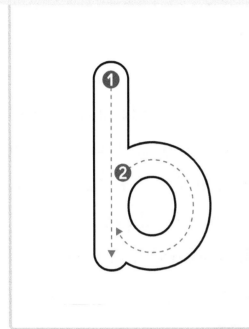

d
I CAN READ

Read the story, and identify and underline all the - d - words.

Daisy's Daring Rescue

Daisy Duck was a dainty, delightful duck. She loved to dance and sing. One day, she heard a dog barking. She decided to go see what was happening. She found a little dog stuck in a ditch. Daisy decided to help him. She dug and dug until the dog was free. The dog was so happy that he gave her a big hug. Daisy smiled and felt proud of herself. She danced and sang with the dog, and they became friends. From that day on, Daisy and the dog went on many adventures together.

read and write

Write all the "d" words you can see in the story			

I CAN READ

Read the sentences and answers the questions: Put a check mark

Denny was a duck

Billy dug a deep hole

Dolly and Denny danced happily

Questions

1. What animal was Denny?   duck ☐   cat ☐
2. Who dug a deep hole?   billy ☐   ava ☐

Write the correct word beside each scrambled word.

dgo ___	dihs ___	depe ___
dda ___	dto ___	donw ___
dya ___	dukc ___	deks ___

Make sentences

Dog
_____
_____

Door
_____
_____

Rules
TRACE AND COLOR

Trace it:

D D D D

d d d d

down down down

Colour it:

I CAN WRITE

Color Me!

dish

Circle the – d – words

fear	anglo	dish
dot	gear	deep
desk	bone	drink

Trace the words

drink   drink
drip   drip
drive   drive

Fill in the missing letters

do ____   duc ____
da ____   dee ____
dis ____ dow ____

Read and Trace the sentence.

I Love my Dad
i love my dad

READ AGAIN

Read the story, and answer each question. highlight the answers in the story.

Daisy's Daring Rescue

Daisy Duck was a dainty, delightful duck. She loved to dance and sing. One day, she heard a dog barking. She decided to go see what was happening. She found a little dog stuck in a ditch. Daisy decided to help him. She dug and dug until the dog was free. The dog was so happy that he gave her a big hug. Daisy smiled and felt proud of herself. She danced and sang with the dog, and they became friends. From that day on, Daisy and the dog went on many adventures together.

Answer Each Question.

1 - What kind of animal was Daisy?
_____

2 - What did Daisy love to do?
_____

3 - What did Daisy do when she found the dog stuck in the ditch?
_____

COLOR ME

Read and color the Letter

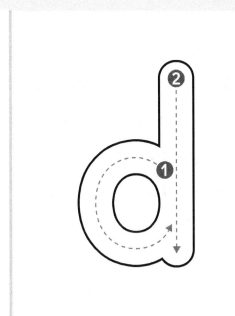
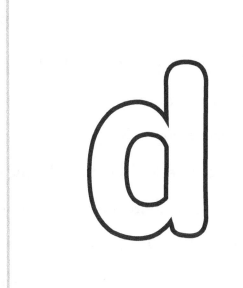

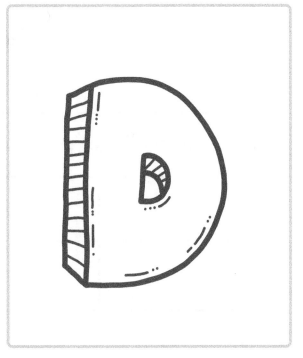

I CAN READ

p

Read the story, and identify and underline all the - p - words.

Penny's Park Rescue

Penny the pig was a playful, plump pig. She loved to run and jump. One day, she saw a pretty purple flower. She picked it and put it in her pocket. She ran into her pal Peter the puppy, who was sad because he lost his ball. Penny wanted to help Peter find his ball, so they searched the park. They looked under the bench, behind the tree, and even in the pond. Finally, they found it in the bush. Peter was so happy that he gave Penny a big hug. Penny smiled, feeling proud of herself for being a good friend.

read and write

Write all the "p" words you can see in the story

I CAN READ

Read the sentences and answers the questions: Put a check mark

Playful pink pig

Pat has a pet puppy

Papa ate a juicy pear

Questions

1. What pet does Pat have?   duck ☐   pet puppy ☐
2. What did Papa eat?   juicy pear ☐   candy ☐

Write the correct word beside each scrambled word.

pna ____	pte ____	pdo ____
pta ____	pgi ____	pti ____
pne ____	pni ____	ppo ____

Make sentences

Pet _____

_____

pat _____

_____

Rules
TRACE AND COLOR

Trace it:

P   P   P   P

p   p   p   p

pin   pin   pin

Colour it:

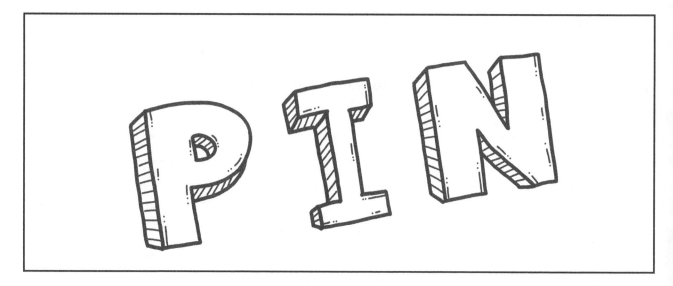

I CAN WRITE

Color Me!

Circle the - p - words

pat	anglo	dish
pet	gear	pow
desk	pit	drink

Trace the words

Fill in the missing letters

pa ___	puf ___
po ___	par ___
pi ___	pizz ___

Read and Trace the sentence.

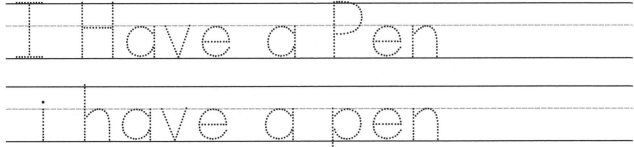

READ AGAIN

Read the story, and answer each question. highlight the answers in the story.

Penny's Park Rescue

Penny the pig was a playful, plump pig. She loved to run and jump. One day, she saw a pretty purple flower. She picked it and put it in her pocket. She ran into her pal Peter the puppy, who was sad because he lost his ball. Penny wanted to help Peter find his ball, so they searched the park. They looked under the bench, behind the tree, and even in the pond. Finally, they found it in the bush. Peter was so happy that he gave Penny a big hug. Penny smiled, feeling proud of herself for being a good friend.

Answer Each Question.

1 - Who did Penny meet in the park?

_____

2 - Why was Peter sad?

_____

3 - Where did they finally find Peter's ball?

_____

COLOR ME

Read and color the Letter

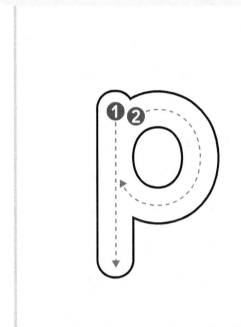

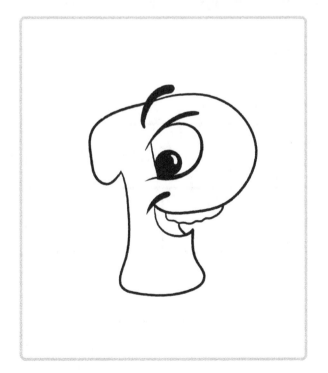

I CAN READ

Read the story, and identify and underline all the - q - words.

Penny's Park Rescue

Once upon a time, there was a funny bird named Quincy. Quincy was always making silly sounds like quacking and quivering. One day, Quincy went on an adventure to find a new feather for his collection. He searched high and low, but all he found were things like quails and quinces. Just when he was about to give up, he heard a soft voice say, "Hello, Quincy! I have just what you're looking for." It was a wise old owl who showed him a beautiful feather that fit perfectly in his collection. Quincy was so happy that he flapped his wings and gave the owl a big hug. From then on, Quincy learned that sometimes you have to keep looking and asking questions to find what you need.

read and write

Write all the "q" words you can see in the story

I CAN READ

Read the sentences and answers the questions: Put a check mark

The rabbit was quick and ran away

The library was so quiet

He decided to quit his job

Questions

1. What did the rabbit do?   play ☐   quick and ran away ☐

2. How was the library?   very quiet ☐   crowded ☐

Write the correct word beside each scrambled word.

quikc ____	quene ____	queeu ____
quiet ____	quartre ____	quoet ____
quitl ____	quets ____	qupi ____

Make sentences

Queen
_____
_____

Quick
_____
_____

20

Rules
TRACE AND COLOR

Trace it:

Q   Q   Q   Q

q   q   q   q

quiet   quiet   quiet

Colour it:

I CAN WRITE

Color Me!

Circle the - q - words

queen	anglo	quick
pet	quip	quilt
quote	pit	quart

Trace the words

quail   quail
quilt   quilt
quiz   quiz

Fill in the missing letters

qui ____   quot ____

quac ____   quar ____

quie ____   ques ____

Read and Trace the sentence.

Quill is very sharp

quill is very sharp

READ AGAIN

Read the story, and answer each question. highlight the answers in the story.

Penny's Park Rescue

Once upon a time, there was a funny bird named Quincy. Quincy was always making silly sounds like quacking and quivering. One day, Quincy went on an adventure to find a new feather for his collection. He searched high and low, but all he found were things like quails and quinces. Just when he was about to give up, he heard a soft voice say, "Hello, Quincy! I have just what you're looking for." It was a wise old owl who showed him a beautiful feather that fit perfectly in his collection. Quincy was so happy that he flapped his wings and gave the owl a big hug. From then on, Quincy learned that sometimes you have to keep looking and asking questions to find what you need.

Answer Each Question.

1- What was Quincy's hobby?

_____

2- Who did Quincy meet on his adventure?

_____

3- What did the wise old owl give Quincy?

_____

COLOR ME

Read and color the Letter

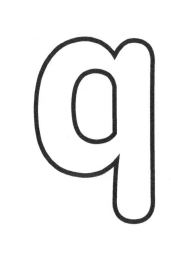

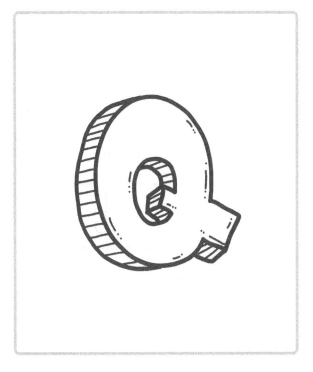

u
I CAN READ

Read the story, and identify and underline all the - u - words.

Umbrella Saves the Day

Bubbles was an inquisitive bunny who lived once upon a time. Bubbles enjoyed jumping and hopping around the fields, discovering new areas and making new friends. Bubbles came across a large umbrella laying on the ground one day while on his expedition. He took it in his hands and began to swirl it around, opening and shutting it. Suddenly, it began to rain! Bubbles recalled the umbrella and opened it immediately to stay dry. As he headed back home, he realized that even a letter "U" in an umbrella may save the day.

read and write

Write all the "u" words you can see in the story

I CAN READ

Read the sentences and answers the questions: Put a check mark

He likes to chew gum

We saw a huge bug

The unicorn has wings

Questions

1. What does the unicorn have?   wings ☐   ball ☐
2. What does he like to chew?   pancake ☐   gum ☐

Write the correct word beside each scrambled word.

undre ———	unifomr ———	usre ———
utensisl ———	uncle ———	urbna ———
uniconr ———	uniqeu ———	usula ———

Make sentences

Under
_____
_____

Uncle
_____
_____

Rules
TRACE AND COLOR

Trace it:

U   U   U   U

u   u   u   u

under under under

Colour it:

I CAN WRITE

Color Me!

usual

Circle the - u - words

ugly   anglo   use

pet   urgent   quilt

utmost   pit   utility

Trace the words

us   us

unique   unique

user   user

Fill in the missing letters

use ____   uniqu ____

umbrell ____   urgen ____

unifor ____   urba ____

Read and Trace the sentence.

We saw a huge bug

We saw a huge bug

READ AGAIN

Read the story, and answer each question. highlight the answers in the story.

Umbrella Saves the Day

Bubbles was an inquisitive bunny who lived once upon a time. Bubbles enjoyed jumping and hopping around the fields, discovering new areas and making new friends. Bubbles came across a large umbrella laying on the ground one day while on his expedition. He took it in his hands and began to swirl it around, opening and shutting it. Suddenly, it began to rain! Bubbles recalled the umbrella and opened it immediately to stay dry. As he headed back home, he realized that even a letter "U" in an umbrella may save the day.

Answer Each Question.

1 - What did Bubbles find while on his expedition?

_____

2 - What did Bubbles do when it started to rain?

_____

3 - What did Bubbles realize as he headed back home?

_____

COLOR ME

Read and color the Letter

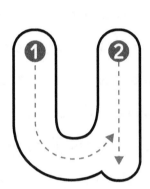

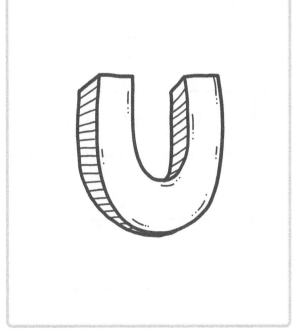

I CAN READ

Read the story, and identify and underline all the - v - words.

Vicky's Valiant Vole Rescue

In a peaceful village, there lived a kind and courageous Viking named Vally. He was known for his valiant deeds and was respected by all. One day, while he was on a voyage, his vessel was caught in a vicious storm. Vally tried to steer his ship through the violent waves, but it was no use. As the storm grew stronger, the ship began to vibrate, and Vally feared it would break into pieces. He quickly gathered his crew and instructed them to use the life vests. They all held onto each other tightly and prayed for their safety. Finally, the storm passed, and the ship remained intact. Vally's bravery and quick thinking saved the day. The crew celebrated their victory and praised Vally's valor. From that day on, Vally was known as the Viking who overcame a violent storm and emerged victorious.

read and write

Write all the "v" words you can see in the story			

I CAN READ

Read the sentences and answers the questions: Put a check mark

The van drove very fast

The volcano is erupting

Violin sounds nice

Questions

1. How did the van drive? Very fast ☐   slowly ☐
2. How does the violin sound? nice ☐   enjoyable ☐

Write the correct word beside each scrambled word.

vna ____	vacumu ____	violni ____
vets ____	vaes ____	villaeg ____
violte ____	vien ____	victoyr ____

Make sentences

Vest _____
_____
_____

Vase _____
_____
_____

Rules
TRACE AND COLOR

Trace it:

V V V V

v v v v

vine vine vine

Colour it:

I CAN WRITE

Color Me!

village

Circle the - v - words

vapor   anglo   vase

pet   venom   quilt

volcano   pit   violin

Trace the words

vacation
volume
vulture

Fill in the missing letters

volum ____   villag ____

violi ____   volcan ____

vapo ____   veno ____

Read and Trace the sentence.

A very big van

a very big van

READ AGAIN

Read the story, and answer each question. highlight the answers in the story.

Vicky's Valiant Vole Rescue

In a peaceful village, there lived a kind and courageous Viking named Vally. He was known for his valiant deeds and was respected by all. One day, while he was on a voyage, his vessel was caught in a vicious storm. Vally tried to steer his ship through the violent waves, but it was no use. As the storm grew stronger, the ship began to vibrate, and Vally feared it would break into pieces. He quickly gathered his crew and instructed them to use the life vests. They all held onto each other tightly and prayed for their safety. Finally, the storm passed, and the ship remained intact. Vally's bravery and quick thinking saved the day. The crew celebrated their victory and praised Vally's valor. From that day on, Vally was known as the Viking who overcame a violent storm and emerged victorious.

Answer Each Question.

1 - Who was Vally in the peaceful village?

_____

2 - What happened to Vally's vessel while he was on a voyage?

_____

3 - How did Vally try to overcome the storm?

_____

COLOR ME

Read and color the Letter

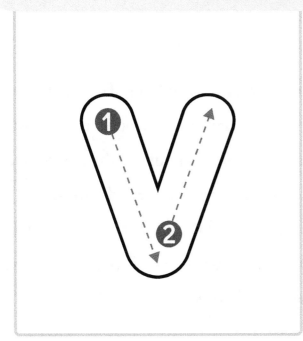
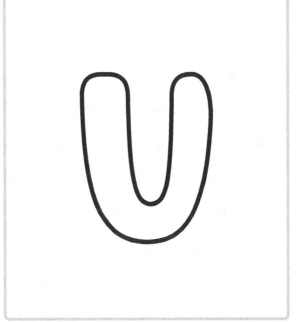

I CAN READ

Read the story, and identify and underline all the - w - words.

Wally and the Wounded Octopus

Wally, the friendly walrus, loved to swim and play with his friends in the wonderful world of water. One day, while wandering through the waves, Wally saw a wounded octopus in need of help. Without hesitation, Wally rushed to the octopus's aid and worked to wrap its wound with a wet washcloth. Wally stayed with the octopus until it felt better and could swim again. The octopus was grateful and became one of Wally's closest friends in the world of water.

read and write

Write all the "w" words you can see in the story			

I CAN READ

Read the sentences and answers the questions: Put a check mark

The dog will wag his tail

Let's play in the wet sand

We cooked noodles in a wok

Questions

1. Where should we play?   the west sand ☐   the garden ☐
2. What did we cook in?   cup ☐   wok ☐

Write the correct word beside each scrambled word.

wni ___	wga ___	wko ___
wgi ___	wbe ___	wxa ___
wte ___	wde ___	wsa ___

Make sentences

Was
_____
_____

Will
_____
_____

Rules
TRACE AND COLOR

Trace it:

W W W W

w w w w

web web web

Colour it:

I CAN WRITE

Color Me!

wolf

Circle the - w - words

vapor	week	vase
pet	venom	wad
wish	wax	violin

Trace the words

Fill in the missing letters

wol ___   wa ___

wee ___   we ___

wok ___   wi ___

Read and Trace the sentence.

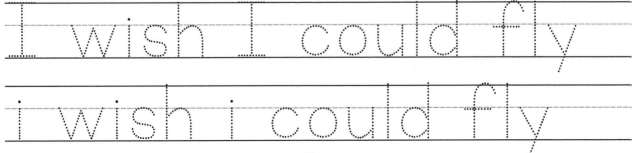

READ AGAIN

Read the story, and answer each question. highlight the answers in the story.

Wally and the Wounded Octopus

Wally, the friendly walrus, loved to swim and play with his friends in the wonderful world of water. One day, while wandering through the waves, Wally saw a wounded octopus in need of help. Without hesitation, Wally rushed to the octopus's aid and worked to wrap its wound with a wet washcloth. Wally stayed with the octopus until it felt better and could swim again. The octopus was grateful and became one of Wally's closest friends in the world of water.

Answer Each Question.

1 - What did Wally see while he was swimming?

_____

2 - Did Wally leave the octopus after helping it?

_____

3 - How did the octopus feel after Wally helped it?

_____

COLOR ME

Read and color the Letter

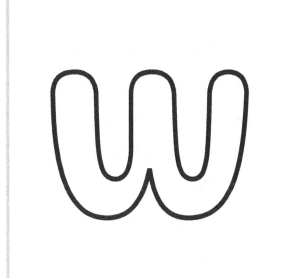
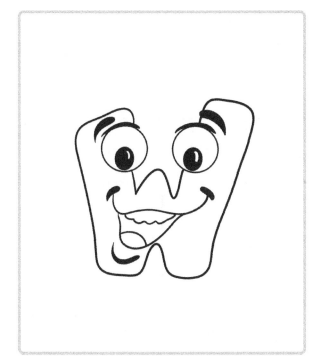

F
I CAN READ

Read the story, and identify and underline all the - f - words.

Finn's Friendly Dolphin

Finn the fish was frightened. He saw a big, fierce shark swimming his way. Finn swam as fast as he could, but the shark was faster. Suddenly, a friendly dolphin appeared and fought off the shark. Finn was safe and felt grateful to the dolphin. They became fast friends and swam together for hours. Finn learned that there were both frightening and friendly creatures in the sea. But with the help of his new friend, he knew he could face anything in the wonderful world of water.

read and write

Write all the " f " words you can see in the story			

I CAN READ

Read the sentences and answers the questions: Put a check mark

A frog jumps high

The fire burns hot

A fox has bushy fur

Questions

1. How does a frog jump?   high ☐   fast ☐
2. What's a fox's fur like?   good ☐   bushy ☐

Write the correct word beside each scrambled word.

fna _____	fyl _____	fihs _____
frgo _____	famr _____	flga _____
fier _____	fxo _____	fodo _____

Make sentences

Fly _____
_____
_____

Fire _____
_____
_____

Rules
TRACE AND COLOR

Trace it:

F F F F

f f f f

fish fish fish

Colour it:

I CAN WRITE

Color Me!

Circle the - f - words

vapor   fun   fish

flag   venom   flower

fur   food   violin

Trace the words

fang   fang
film   film
food   food

Fill in the missing letters

fir ____   fla ____

fro ____   flowe ____

fis ____   fan ____

Read and Trace the sentence.

A fang is sharp

a fang is sharp

READ AGAIN

Read the story, and answer each question. highlight the answers in the story.

Finn's Friendly Dolphin

Finn the fish was frightened. He saw a big, fierce shark swimming his way. Finn swam as fast as he could, but the shark was faster. Suddenly, a friendly dolphin appeared and fought off the shark. Finn was safe and felt grateful to the dolphin. They became fast friends and swam together for hours. Finn learned that there were both frightening and friendly creatures in the sea. But with the help of his new friend, he knew he could face anything in the wonderful world of water.

Answer Each Question.

1 - Who frightened Finn?

_____

2 - Who saved Finn from the shark?

_____

3 - How did Finn feel after the dolphin saved him?

_____

COLOR ME

Read and color the Letter

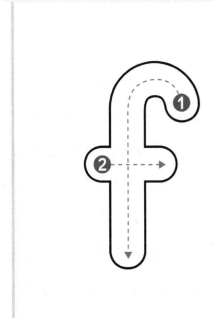

t

I CAN READ

Read the story, and identify and underline all the - t - words.

Timmy's Smart Cat

Timmy sat on his mat and looked at his pet cat. The cat sat on his lap and purred. Timmy stroked the cat and felt happy. He saw a bug and tried to catch it, but it was too quick. The cat saw Timmy's game and jumped off his lap. She ran and caught the bug in her mouth! Timmy ran to tell his mom about his cat's catch. She smiled and said, "Your cat is very smart!" Timmy beamed with pride and hugged his cat. They played together until it was time for dinner, He loved his cat and was glad she was so fast.

read and write

Write all the " t " words you can see in the story

I CAN READ

Read the sentences and answers the questions: Put a check mark

Ten birds flew over Timmy

Two boys played together

Tie your shoes, Timmy

Questions

1. How many birds flew over Timmy?   ten ☐   one ☐
2. How many boys played together?   two ☐   three ☐

Write the correct word beside each scrambled word.

tbu ____	tpo ____	tow ____
tyo ____	tpa ____	tni ____
tne ____	tga ____	tda ____

Make sentences

Toy _____
_____
_____

Tea _____
_____
_____

Rules
TRACE AND COLOR

Trace it:

T T T T

t t t t

top top top

Colour it:

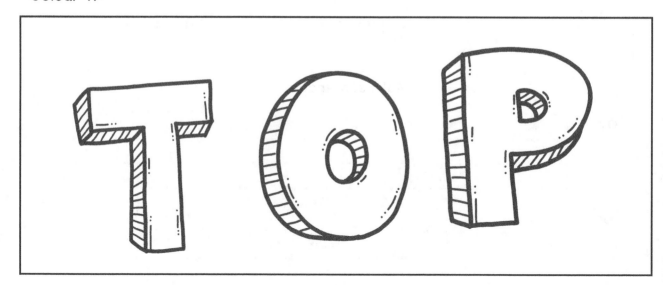

I CAN WRITE

Color Me!

Circle the - t - words

vapor	tab	fish
tan	venom	tip
tag	tea	violin

Trace the words

tag   tag
tap   tap
ten   ten

Fill in the missing letters

ta ___   tu ___
to ___   ta ___
te ___   to ___

Read and Trace the sentence.

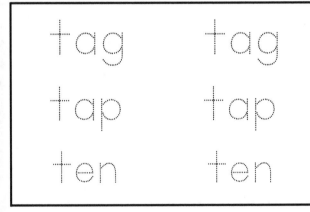

Tie your shoes
Tie your shoes

READ AGAIN

Read the story, and answer each question. highlight the answers in the story.

Timmy's Smart Cat

Timmy sat on his mat and looked at his pet cat. The cat sat on his lap and purred. Timmy stroked the cat and felt happy. He saw a bug and tried to catch it, but it was too quick. The cat saw Timmy's game and jumped off his lap. She ran and caught the bug in her mouth! Timmy ran to tell his mom about his cat's catch. She smiled and said, "Your cat is very smart!" Timmy beamed with pride and hugged his cat. They played together until it was time for dinner, He loved his cat and was glad she was so fast.

Answer Each Question.

1 - What did Timmy try to catch?

_____

2 - Who did Timmy tell about the catch?

_____

3 - What did Timmy's mom say about the cat?

_____

COLOR ME

Read and color the Letter

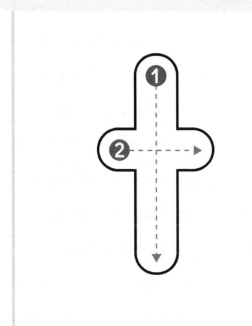

m
I CAN READ

Read the story, and identify and underline all the - m - words.

Mischievous Monkey Max

Once upon a time, there was a mischievous monkey named Max. Max loved to climb trees and play tricks on his animal friends in the jungle. One day, Max saw a mango tree with lots of juicy mangoes. He wanted to eat them all but he knew he couldn't climb the tree by himself. So, he had an idea. Max ran to his friend, a mighty elephant named Emma. Max asked Emma if she could lift him up to the mango tree. Emma agreed and lifted Max up with her strong trunk. Max quickly picked as many mangoes as he could carry and climbed back down. He thanked Emma and shared some mangoes with her. From that day on, Max knew he could always count on his friends in the jungle.

read and write

Write all the " m " words you can see in the story			

I CAN READ

Read the sentences and answers the questions: Put a check mark

Mandy's magic show amazed everyone

The moon is big

My mouse is brown

Questions

1. Is the moon big or small?   big ☐   small ☐
2. What color is my mouse?   blue ☐   brown ☐

Write the correct word beside each scrambled word.

mono ____	mdu ____	movei ____
moues ____	mxa ____	monkye ____
manog ____	musci ____	mpa ____

Make sentences

Map
_____
_____

Magic
_____
_____

Rules
TRACE AND COLOR

Trace it:

M M M M

m m m m

milk milk milk

Colour it:

I CAN WRITE

Color Me!

movie

Circle the – m – words

music   tab   fish

tan   monkey   mud

tag   muffin   violin

Trace the words

max   max
mud   mud
map   map

Fill in the missing letters

movi ____   musi ____

mang ____   muffi ____

magi ____   mailbo ____

Read and Trace the sentence.

Molly has toys

molly has toys

READ AGAIN

Read the story, and answer each question. highlight the answers in the story.

Mischievous Monkey Max

Once upon a time, there was a mischievous monkey named Max. Max loved to climb trees and play tricks on his animal friends in the jungle. One day, Max saw a mango tree with lots of juicy mangoes. He wanted to eat them all but he knew he couldn't climb the tree by himself. So, he had an idea. Max ran to his friend, a mighty elephant named Emma. Max asked Emma if she could lift him up to the mango tree. Emma agreed and lifted Max up with her strong trunk. Max quickly picked as many mangoes as he could carry and climbed back down. He thanked Emma and shared some mangoes with her. From that day on, Max knew he could always count on his friends in the jungle.

Answer Each Question.

1 - What did Max love to do in the jungle?
_____

2 - What did Max see in the jungle one day?
_____

3 - Who helped Max get the mangoes down?
_____

COLOR ME

Read and color the Letter

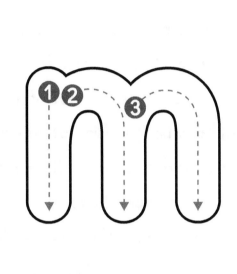
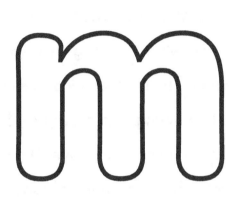
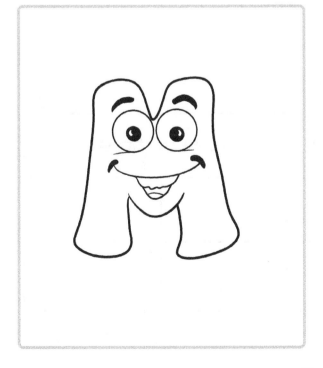
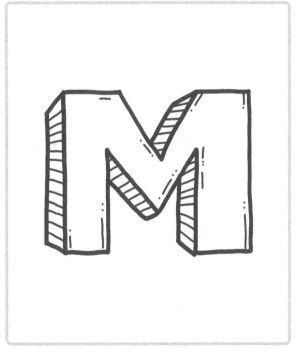

I CAN READ

Read the story, and identify and underline all the - n - words.

The Kind Fox

Of all the creatures in the land, none were more nimble than Nia, the fox. With her sleek fur and quick mind, Nia could outrun any foe. One day, while prowling through the woods, Nia came upon a nest of tiny birds. The mother bird, a kind soul named Nina, begged Nia not to harm her young. Nia, moved by Nina's plea, promised to protect the nest from harm. For days, Nia stood guard over the nest, keeping watch until the birds were strong enough to fly away. From that day on, Nia was known not only for her speed, but also for her kindness.

read and write

Write all the " n " words you can see in the story

I CAN READ

Read the sentences and answers the questions: Put a check mark

All the hens ate bread

Nan saw nell smile happily

He saw no more newts

Questions

1. What did all the hens eat?   brad ☐   pizza ☐
2. What did nan see nell do?   smile happily ☐   angry ☐

Write the correct word beside each scrambled word.

nobel ___	naem ___	ntu ___
nera ___	narrwo ___	noes ___
norht ___	neta ___	npa ___

Make sentences

Nap _____

_____

Nut _____

_____

Rules
TRACE AND COLOR

Trace it:

N   N   N   N

n   n   n   n

nest   nest   nest

Colour it:

I CAN WRITE

Color Me!

nose

Circle the - n - words

name	tab	neat
tan	nose	nap
tag	nibble	violin

Trace the words

nap   nap
night night
nun   nun

Fill in the missing letters

nu ____   nugge ____

nort ____   nav ____

necta ____   napki ____

Read and Trace the sentence.

Nods and naps

nods and naps

READ AGAIN

Read the story, and answer each question. highlight the answers in the story.

The Kind Fox

Of all the creatures in the land, none were more nimble than Nia, the fox. With her sleek fur and quick mind, Nia could outrun any foe. One day, while prowling through the woods, Nia came upon a nest of tiny birds. The mother bird, a kind soul named Nina, begged Nia not to harm her young. Nia, moved by Nina's plea, promised to protect the nest from harm. For days, Nia stood guard over the nest, keeping watch until the birds were strong enough to fly away. From that day on, Nia was known not only for her speed, but also for her kindness.

Answer Each Question.

1- What did Nia come across in the woods?
_____

2 - What did Nina ask of Nia?
_____

3 - What did Nia promise Nina?
_____

COLOR ME

Read and color the Letter

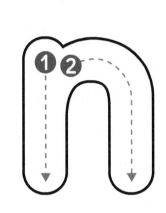

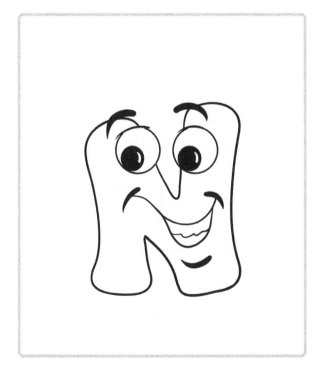

I CAN READ

Read the story, and identify and underline all the - x - words.

Box Adventure Fun

Six foxes shared a large box. They enjoyed playing and having fun, but they were always getting into mischief. They ran and jumped over rocks and logs in the nearby woods one day. They soon became disoriented. They looked for a way back but found only tall trees and bushes. They were startled to hear a howl. It turned out to be a wolf! They ran until they came across a path. It brought them back to their box. They had a picnic and played soccer the next day. The yellow fox triumphed with a deft shot. The foxes snuggled into their soft box as the sun set. Except for the crickets chirping outside, the night was quiet. The foxes dozed off, dreaming of their

read and write

Write all the " x " words you can see in the story			

I CAN READ

Read the sentences and answers the questions: Put a check mark

The box is big and heavy

Texas is a big state

The boxer won the match

Questions

1. How would you describe Texas?   tall ☐   big state ☐
2. What are the characteristics of the box?   small ☐   big and heavy ☐

Write the correct word beside each scrambled word.

bxo _____	wxa _____	extar _____
fxo _____	netx _____	boxre _____
fxi _____	texsa _____	flxe _____

Make sentences

Six _____

Ox _____

Rules
TRACE AND COLOR

Trace it:

X　　X　　X　　X

x　　x　　x　　x

text　text　text

Colour it:

I CAN WRITE

Color Me!

Circle the - x - words

flex	max	neat
ox	nose	pixel
tag	six	tax

Trace the words

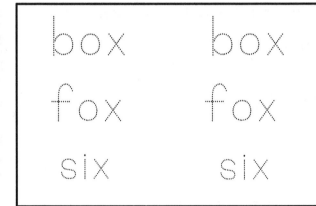

Fill in the missing letters

nu ____   nugge ____

nort ____   nav ____

necta ____   napki ____

Read and Trace the sentence.

I have a box
I have a box

70

READ AGAIN

Read the story, and answer each question. highlight the answers in the story.

Box Adventure Fun

Six foxes shared a large box. They enjoyed playing and having fun, but they were always getting into mischief. They ran and jumped over rocks and logs in the nearby woods one day. They soon became disoriented. They looked for a way back but found only tall trees and bushes. They were startled to hear a howl. It turned out to be a wolf! They ran until they came across a path. It brought them back to their box. They had a picnic and played soccer the next day. The yellow fox triumphed with a deft shot. The foxes snuggled into their soft box as the sun set. Except for the crickets chirping outside, the night was quiet. The foxes dozed off, dreaming of their

Answer Each Question.

1 - How many foxes shared the box?

_____

2 - What happened to the foxes while playing in the woods?

_____

3 - Who won the soccer game?

_____

COLOR ME

Read and color the Letter

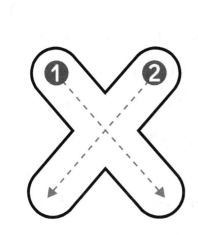
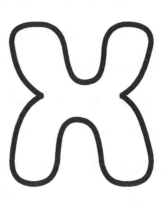

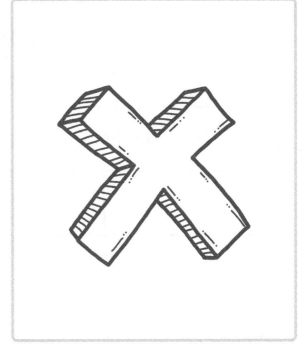

I CAN READ

Read the story, and identify and underline all the - y - words.

Yawning Yellow Yak

Yara the young yellow yak was feeling a bit yucky. She had eaten too many yellow yams, and her tummy was upset. She went to the yard to find some yarrow, a plant known to make yucky tummies feel better. She searched high and low and finally found a patch of yellow yarrow. She ate some and felt much better. As she lay down in the yard, she noticed a beautiful butterfly with yellow and purple wings. The butterfly flew around Yara, and she felt happy. She said, "Thank you, butterfly, for making me feel less yucky." The butterfly fluttered away, and Yara fell asleep, dreaming of yellow yams and colorful butterflies.

read and write

Write all the " y " words you can see in the story			

I CAN READ

Read the sentences and answers the questions: Put a check mark

The yellow yacht sailed across the yard

Yara the young loved to yawn

I love to play with my yo-yo

Questions

1. What sailed across the yard?   car ☐   The yellow yacht ☐
2. Who loved to yawn?   jack ☐   yara ☐

Write the correct word beside each scrambled word.

yka _____	yellwo _____	yokl _____
yanr _____	yadr _____	yeit _____
yanw _____	yma _____	yeanr _____

Make sentences

Yellow _____
_____

Yard _____
_____

Rules
TRACE AND COLOR

Trace it:

Y　　Y　　Y　　Y

y　　y　　y　　y

yolk　yolk　yolk

Colour it:

I CAN WRITE

Color Me!

Circle the - y - words

yam	max	neat
yard	nose	yuck
young	yearn	tax

Trace the words

Fill in the missing letters

yet ____   youn ____

yaw ____   year ____

yol ____   yach ____

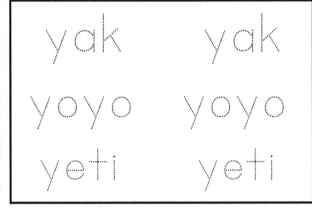

Read and Trace the sentence.

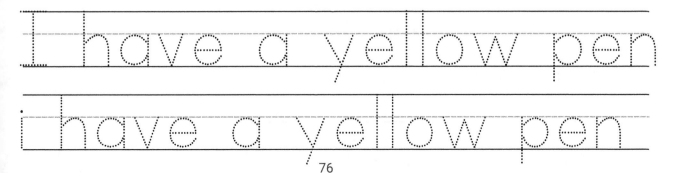

READ AGAIN

Read the story, and answer each question. highlight the answers in the story.

Yawning Yellow Yak

Yara the young yellow yak was feeling a bit yucky. She had eaten too many yellow yams, and her tummy was upset. She went to the yard to find some yarrow, a plant known to make yucky tummies feel better. She searched high and low and finally found a patch of yellow yarrow. She ate some and felt much better. As she lay down in the yard, she noticed a beautiful butterfly with yellow and purple wings. The butterfly flew around Yara, and she felt happy. She said, "Thank you, butterfly, for making me feel less yucky." The butterfly fluttered away, and Yara fell asleep, dreaming of yellow yams and colorful butterflies.

Answer Each Question.

1 - What did Yara eat too much of?

_____

2 - What did Yara look for in the yard?

_____

3 - What did Yara dream about?

_____

COLOR ME

Read and color the Letter

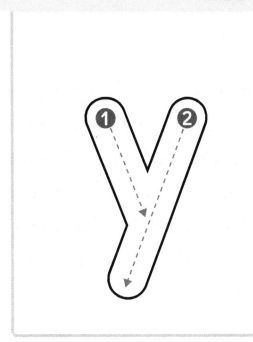
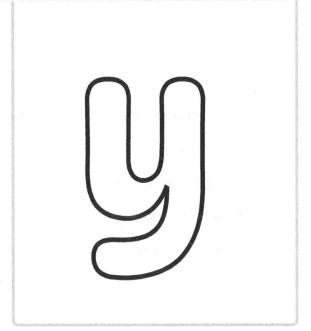

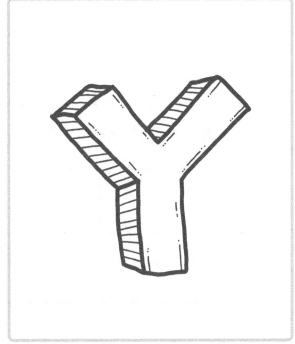

I CAN READ

Read the story, and identify and underline all the - z - words.

Zippy Zebra's Adventure

Zack was a zippy zebra. He loved to zoom around the zoo, zigzagging through the trees. One day, while Zach was napping in the sun, a buzzing sound woke him up. He looked up and saw a big, buzzing bee! The bee was zooming toward Zach, but Zach didn't zip away. Instead, he held still and watched the bee as it buzzed around him. The bee landed on Zach's nose and Zach sneezed, sending the bee flying away. Zach zipped away, feeling zany and happy.

read and write

Write all the " z " words you can see in the story			

I CAN READ

Read the sentences and answers the questions: Put a check mark

The zebra ran through the zoo

The sauce was very zesty

The path went zigzag

Questions

1. What did the zebra do in the zoo? play ☐   ran ☐
2. What was the sauce like? spicy ☐   very zesty ☐

Write the correct word beside each scrambled word.

zpi ____	zigzga ____	maez ____
zebar ____	zayn ____	glaez ____
zeor ____	zomo ____	fuzyz ____

Make sentences

Zoo
_____
_____

Zero
_____
_____

Rules
TRACE AND COLOR

Trace it:

Z Z Z Z

Z Z Z Z

zero zero zero

Colour it:

I CAN WRITE

Color Me!

maze

Circle the - z - words

yam	maze	neat
daze	nose	glaze
buzz	yearn	lazy

Trace the words

zip   zip
zoo   zoo
zany   zany

Fill in the missing letters

zan ____   zan ____

priz ____   zest ____

fuzz ____   freez ____

Read and Trace the sentence.

Zebra in the zoo

zebra in the zoo

READ AGAIN

Read the story, and answer each question. highlight the answers in the story.

Zippy Zebra's Adventure

Zack was a zippy zebra. He loved to zoom around the zoo, zigzagging through the trees. One day, while Zach was napping in the sun, a buzzing sound woke him up. He looked up and saw a big, buzzing bee! The bee was zooming toward Zach, but Zach didn't zip away. Instead, he held still and watched the bee as it buzzed around him. The bee landed on Zach's nose and Zach sneezed, sending the bee flying away. Zach zipped away, feeling zany and happy.

Answer Each Question.

1 - What animal is Zack?
_____

2 - What woke Zack up from his nap?
_____

3 - How did Zack feel after the bee flew away?
_____

COLOR ME

Read and color the Letter

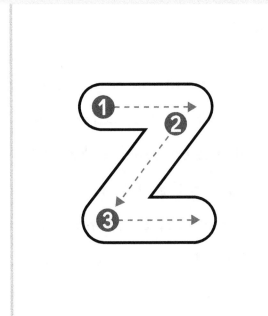

I CAN READ

br

Read the story, and identify and underline all the - br - words.

Bunny's Brave Beach

Brad the brave bunny loved to explore. He went to the bright, breezy beach one day. He brought a blue ball with him to play catch. Brad threw the ball high and it flew away with the breeze! He chased it bravely, but it was too fast. He saw a bridge in the distance, and ran towards it. He crossed the bridge and found his ball, stuck in a branch. Brad was happy to have his ball back and decided to head back home, feeling proud of his bravery.

read and write

Write all the " br " words you can see in the story

I CAN READ

Read the sentences and answers the questions: Put a check mark

The house was made of brick

The bridge led to a park

The brain helps us think

Questions

1. What was the house made of?   brick ☐   carton ☐
2. How does the brain help us?   think ☐   play ☐

Write the correct word beside each scrambled word.

branhc _____	brideg _____	brani _____
bronw _____	brmi _____	bruhs _____
bromo _____	bradi _____	breaht _____

Make sentences

Brain
_____
_____

Brave
_____
_____

Rules
TRACE AND COLOR

Trace it:

BR BR BR BR

br br br br

brave brave

Colour it:

I CAN WRITE

Color Me!

brim

Circle the - br - words

yam	brim	neat
daze	brown	brush
broth	yearn	braid

Trace the words

braid braid
bright bright
brush brush

Fill in the missing letters

brus ____   brid ____

breat ____   brai ____

brow ____   bric ____

Read and Trace the sentence.

He eats breakfast
he eats breakfast

READ AGAIN

Read the story, and answer each question. highlight the answers in the story.

Bunny's Brave Beach

Brad the brave bunny loved to explore. He went to the bright, breezy beach one day. He brought a blue ball with him to play catch. Brad threw the ball high and it flew away with the breeze! He chased it bravely, but it was too fast. He saw a bridge in the distance, and ran towards it. He crossed the bridge and found his ball, stuck in a branch. Brad was happy to have his ball back and decided to head back home, feeling proud of his bravery.

Answer Each Question.

1 - What did Brad bring to the beach?
_____

2 - Did Brad find his ball?
_____

3 - Where did Brad find his ball?
_____

COLOR ME

Read and color the Letter

pl
I CAN READ

Read the story, and identify and underline all the - pl - words.

Polly's Playful Plum

Polly the playful polar bear loved to play in the snow. One day, she found a plump, purple plum in the snow. She picked it up and wondered what it was. Polly decided to ask her friend Pete the penguin. She asked Pete if he knew what the plump, purple plum was. Pete said, "That's not a plum, Polly. It's a plastic ball!" Polly was surprised, but still decided to play with the plastic ball. She and Pete played together until it was time for Polly to go back to her igloo. Polly went to sleep, dreaming of more playful adventures in the snow.

read and write

Write all the " pl " words you can see in the story			

I CAN READ

Read the sentences and answers the questions: Put a check mark

We planted some flowers

Plug in the lamp

The rock went plop

Questions

1. What did you plant? floewrs ☐   tomato ☐
2. What should you plug in? lamp ☐   car ☐

Write the correct word beside each scrambled word.

plya _____	plaet _____	plupm _____
plmu _____	platn _____	plto _____
pleaes _____	plsu _____	pladi _____

Make sentences

Play _____

_____

Plate _____

_____

Rules
TRACE AND COLOR

Trace it:

PL PL PL PL

pl pl pl pl

plop   plop

Colour it:

I CAN WRITE

Color Me!

plus

Circle the – pl – words

plus	brim	neat
plug	plenty	brush
broth	plaid	braid

Trace the words

play   play
plum   plum
plug   plug

Fill in the missing letters

playe ____   plai ____

plier ____   plasti ____

plane ____   plat ____

Read and Trace the sentence.

Pluto is far away
Pluto is far away

READ AGAIN

Read the story, and answer each question. highlight the answers in the story.

Polly's Playful Plum

Polly the playful polar bear loved to play in the snow. One day, she found a plump, purple plum in the snow. She picked it up and wondered what it was. Polly decided to ask her friend Pete the penguin. She asked Pete if he knew what the plump, purple plum was. Pete said, "That's not a plum, Polly. It's a plastic ball!" Polly was surprised, but still decided to play with the plastic ball. She and Pete played together until it was time for Polly to go back to her igloo. Polly went to sleep, dreaming of more playful adventures in the snow.

Answer Each Question.

1- Who found the plum?
_____

2 - What did Polly ask Pete?
_____

3 - What did Pete say it was?
_____

COLOR ME

Read and color the Letter

I CAN READ

bl

Read the story, and identify and underline all the - bl - words.

Blue Balloon Adventure

Benny the blue bird had a big blue balloon. One bright day, Benny decided to fly high up into the blue sky with his balloon. As he flew, he saw a big, black bug on a blooming bluebell. Benny felt brave and flew closer to the bug to say hello. Suddenly, a blast of wind blew Benny and his balloon away. Benny felt scared, but he held onto the balloon tightly. Luckily, the balloon didn't burst and he landed safely on a nearby branch. Benny was relieved and decided to go back home, but he knew he would always remember his exciting adventure in the blue sky.

read and write

Write all the " bl " words you can see in the story			

I CAN READ

Read the sentences and answers the questions: Put a check mark

The blue balloon floated

The fire blazed brightly

The blender whirred loudly

Questions

1. What did the blue balloon do?   floated ☐   stopping ☐
2. What sound did the blender make?   whirred ☐   noises ☐

Write the correct word beside each scrambled word.

bleu ____	blaez ____	blikn ____
bluhs ____	blats ____	blipm ____
blakc ____	blaez ____	blaem ____

Make sentences

Blue
_____
_____

Blender
_____
_____

Rules
TRACE AND COLOR

Trace it:

BL BL BL BL

bl bl bl bl

black   black

Colour it:

I CAN WRITE

Color Me!

blink

Circle the - bl - words

blink	brim	blush
daze	blaze	blimp
block	yearn	blurt

Trace the words

blurt   blurt
blaze   blaze
blink   blink

Fill in the missing letters

blende ____   bloc ____
blun ____   bliste ____
blim ____   blam ____

Read and Trace the sentence.

The cat was black
the cat was black

READ AGAIN

Read the story, and answer each question. highlight the answers in the story.

Blue Balloon Adventure

Benny the blue bird had a big blue balloon. One bright day, Benny decided to fly high up into the blue sky with his balloon. As he flew, he saw a big, black bug on a blooming bluebell. Benny felt brave and flew closer to the bug to say hello. Suddenly, a blast of wind blew Benny and his balloon away. Benny felt scared, but he held onto the balloon tightly. Luckily, the balloon didn't burst and he landed safely on a nearby branch. Benny was relieved and decided to go back home, but he knew he would always remember his exciting adventure in the blue sky.

Answer Each Question.

1 - Who had a big blue balloon?
_____

2 - How did Benny feel when he was blown away?
_____

3 - Did Benny's balloon burst?
_____

COLOR ME

Read and color the Letter

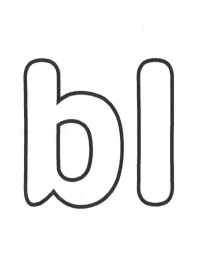

dr
I CAN READ

Read the story, and identify and underline all the - dr - words.

Dr. Dragon's Dream

Dr. Dresser was a fashionable doctor. She loved to wear pretty dresses and shiny jewelry. One day, she noticed that her friend, Mr. Dragon, was feeling sad. She asked him why and he said he wanted to look fashionable too, but he didn't know how to dress up. Dr. Dresser knew just what to do. She took Mr. Dragon to her closet and let him try on some of her dresses and accessories. She helped him pick out a cool outfit that suited him. Mr. Dragon was so happy with his new look that he danced around in excitement. Dr. Dresser realized that helping others feel good about themselves was another way of being a doctor.

read and write

Write all the " dr " words you can see in the story			

I CAN READ

Read the sentences and answers the questions: Put a check mark

The dragon roared loudly

The dresser was pink

The boy had dreams

Questions

1. How did the dragon sound?   loudly ☐   funny ☐
2. What did the boy have?   dreams ☐   book ☐

Write the correct word beside each scrambled word.

dressre ———	drikn ———	dredeg ———
drmu ———	driev ———	dreda ———
drema ———	drwa ———	drivre ———

Make sentences

Draw
_____
_____

Dress
_____
_____

Rules
TRACE AND COLOR

Trace it:

DR DR DR DR

dr dr dr dr

drive   drive

Colour it:

I CAN WRITE

Color Me!

drop

Circle the - dr - words

blink	drop	drift
dress	driver	blimp
block	droop	blurt

Trace the words

dress dress
droll droll
drop   drop

Fill in the missing letters

drop ____   drin ____

dra ____   dru ____

dres ____   drea ____

Read and Trace the sentence.

I drank water
I drank water

READ AGAIN

Read the story, and answer each question. highlight the answers in the story.

Dr. Dragon's Dream

Dr. Dresser was a fashionable doctor. She loved to wear pretty dresses and shiny jewelry. One day, she noticed that her friend, Mr. Dragon, was feeling sad. She asked him why and he said he wanted to look fashionable too, but he didn't know how to dress up. Dr. Dresser knew just what to do. She took Mr. Dragon to her closet and let him try on some of her dresses and accessories. She helped him pick out a cool outfit that suited him. Mr. Dragon was so happy with his new look that he danced around in excitement. Dr. Dresser realized that helping others feel good about themselves was another way of being a doctor.

Answer Each Question.

1 - What's Mr. Dragon's problem?
_____

2 - What did Mr. Dragon say?
_____

3 - How did Dr. Dresser help?
_____

COLOR ME

Read and color the Letter

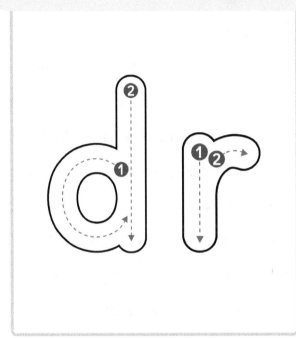

ph
I CAN READ

Read the story, and identify and underline all the - ph - words.

Journey of Discovery

A wise philosopher named Phineas decided to photograph a rare phenomenon he had read about in an ancient book one day. He took his phone and went to the nearest pharmacy to develop the film. While he waited, he overheard a young boy with a needle phobia discussing a vaccine with his doctor. Phineas knew he had to pitch in. He approached the boy and offered to talk about overcoming fear with him. They devised a phrase to repeat during the vaccine, and the boy was brave enough to receive it. Phineas was moved and inspired by the power of philanthropy.

read and write

Write all the " ph " words you can see in the story

I CAN READ

Read the sentences and answers the questions: Put a check mark

The phone rings loudly

I drew a photo

We went to pharmacy

Questions

1. What makes a noise?   phone ☐   car ☐
2. What did you draw?   cat ☐   photo ☐

Write the correct word beside each scrambled word.

phoen ____	phaes ____	phli ____
phoot ____	phto ____	phwe ____
phraes ____	physisc ____	phta ____

Make sentences

Phrase
_____
_____

Phone
_____
_____

Rules
TRACE AND COLOR

Trace it:

PH PH PH PH

ph ph ph ph

photo photo

Colour it:

I CAN WRITE

Color Me!

phase

Circle the - ph - words

phat	drop	phew
phat	driver	phiz
block	droop	phase

Trace the words

phew phew
phone phone
phrase phrase

Fill in the missing letters

phas ____   phonic ____

pharao ____   physic ____

phobi ____   phot ____

Read and Trace the sentence.

Moon is a phase
moon is a phase

READ AGAIN

Read the story, and answer each question. highlight the answers in the story.

Journey of Discovery

A wise philosopher named Phineas decided to photograph a rare phenomenon he had read about in an ancient book one day. He took his phone and went to the nearest pharmacy to develop the film. While he waited, he overheard a young boy with a needle phobia discussing a vaccine with his doctor. Phineas knew he had to pitch in. He approached the boy and offered to talk about overcoming fear with him. They devised a phrase to repeat during the vaccine, and the boy was brave enough to receive it. Phineas was moved and inspired by the power of philanthropy.

Answer Each Question.

1 - Who decided to photograph a rare phenomenon?
_____

2 - Where did the wise philosopher go to develop the film?
_____

3 - How did the boy feel after receiving the vaccine?
_____

COLOR ME

Read and color the Letter

qu
I CAN READ

Read the story, and identify and underline all the - qu - words.

Journey of Discovery

Once upon a time, in a quaint little village, there lived a happy little duck named Quack. He was known for his quick waddling and his love for taking long swims in the nearby pond. One day, he came across a beautiful quilt made of various fabrics. He felt the urge to have it, but he needed to pass a quiz to win it. The quiz was tough, but Quack was determined to win the quilt. He had to be quiet and listen carefully to the questions. He managed to answer them correctly and won the quilt. The villagers were impressed and set a new quota for more quizzes. Quack felt proud, and his tail feather quivered with excitement. He proudly quoted, "Quack, quack, I won the quiz."

read and write

Write all the " qu " words you can see in the story

I CAN READ

Read the sentences and answers the questions: Put a check mark

My grandma made a quilt

I love taking quizzes

The teacher set a quota

Questions

1. Who made the quilt?   grandma ☐   mom ☐
2. What do you love?   quizzes ☐   dogs ☐

Write the correct word beside each scrambled word.

quikc _____   quite _____   qupi _____

quitl _____   quoat _____   quartre _____

quzi _____   quivre _____   qualm _____

Make sentences

Quick
_____
_____

Quiz
_____
_____

Rules
TRACE AND COLOR

Trace it:

Qu Qu Qu Qu

qu qu qu qu

quiet quiet

Colour it:

I CAN WRITE

Color Me!

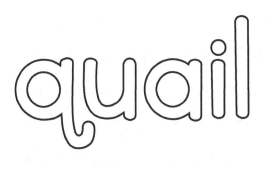

Circle the - qu - words

quail	drop	quiz
phat	quota	phiz
quiver	droop	phase

Trace the words

quail   quail
quest   quest
qualm   qualm

Fill in the missing letters

qual ____   quie ____

quive ____   quenc ____

quarte ____   quot ____

Read and Trace the sentence.

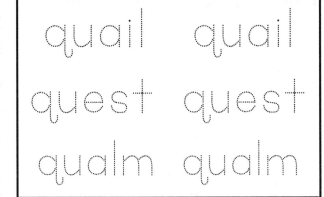

READ AGAIN

Read the story, and answer each question. highlight the answers in the story.

Journey of Discovery

Once upon a time, in a quaint little village, there lived a happy little duck named Quack. He was known for his quick waddling and his love for taking long swims in the nearby pond. One day, he came across a beautiful quilt made of various fabrics. He felt the urge to have it, but he needed to pass a quiz to win it. The quiz was tough, but Quack was determined to win the quilt. He had to be quiet and listen carefully to the questions. He managed to answer them correctly and won the quilt. The villagers were impressed and set a new quota for more quizzes. Quack felt proud, and his tail feather quivered with excitement. He proudly quoted, "Quack, quack, I won the quiz."

Answer Each Question.

1 - What was the name of the duck?

_____

2 - What did Quack come across?

_____

3 - How did Quack feel after winning the quiz?

_____

COLOR ME

Read and color the Letter

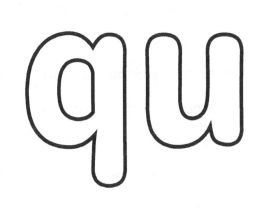

sp
I CAN READ

Read the story, and identify and underline all the - sp - words.

Tangled Web Rescued

Sammy Spider enjoyed spinning webs. He would work for hours on his intricate designs. He spotted a juicy fly while spinning his web one day. He spun around quickly and pounced on the fly. He was about to eat when he realized his web had become tangled. He attempted to spin his way out, but it was futile. A friendly sparrow flew by and noticed Sammy's predicament. She set him free with a quick peck of her beak. Sammy was so touched that he invited the sparrow to join him for dinner. As the sun set behind them, they ate their meal together.

read and write

Write all the " sp " words you can see in the story

I CAN READ

Read the sentences and answers the questions: Put a check mark

The spider can spin webs

I see a spot there

I like mashed spuds

Questions

1. Can the spider spin webs?   yes ☐   no ☐
2. What's your favorite spud dish?   mashed spuds ☐   pizza ☐

Write the correct word beside each scrambled word.

spni _____   spaed _____   spede _____

spto _____   spta _____   spotu _____

spdu _____   spekc _____   splahs _____

Make sentences

Spot
_____
_____

Span
_____
_____

Rules
TRACE AND COLOR

Trace it:

SP SP SP SP

sp sp sp sp

spud spud

Colour it:

I CAN WRITE

Color Me!

span

Circle the - sp - words

quail	span	spool
spill	spicy	phiz
spiny	droop	phase

Trace the words

spin   spin
spot   spot
spill spill

Fill in the missing letters

spu ___   spic ___
spa ___   spide ___
spec ___   spou ___

Read and Trace the sentence.

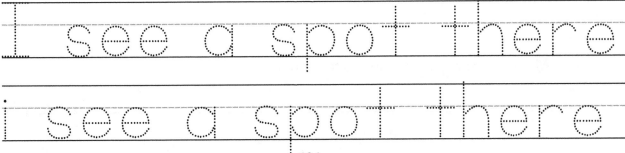

READ AGAIN

Read the story, and answer each question. highlight the answers in the story.

Tangled Web Rescued

Sammy Spider enjoyed spinning webs. He would work for hours on his intricate designs. He spotted a juicy fly while spinning his web one day. He spun around quickly and pounced on the fly. He was about to eat when he realized his web had become tangled. He attempted to spin his way out, but it was futile. A friendly sparrow flew by and noticed Sammy's predicament. She set him free with a quick peck of her beak. Sammy was so touched that he invited the sparrow to join him for dinner. As the sun set behind them, they ate their meal together.

Answer Each Question.

1 - What did Sammy Spider enjoy doing?
_____

2 - What happened to Sammy Spider's web?
_____

3 - Who did Sammy Spider invite to dinner?
_____

COLOR ME

Read and color the Letter

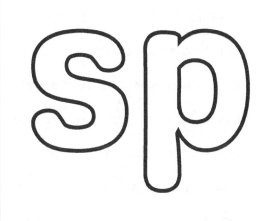

sc
I CAN READ

Read the story, and identify and underline all the - sc - words.

Brave Adventures in Nature

The nearby woods were a favorite place for Lila to explore. She decided to go for a scoop of water after spotting a small stream one day. She knelt down and saw a little rascal taking some berries from a bush close by. She turned when she heard a sudden, loud screech and noticed a bird flying overhead. She felt a little frightened, but then she recalled how brave she had been when she and her friends had gone on a scout trip. She observed the bird fly away while taking a proud stance. Lila felt good about herself and carried on with her journey, confident that she could face anything with courage and confidence.

read and write

Write all the " sc " words you can see in the story

I CAN READ

Read the sentences and answers the questions: Put a check mark

Let's scan the picture for clues

Don't scold your little sister

I used a spoon to scoop the ice cream

Questions

1. Who shouldn't you scold?   sister ☐   cat ☐
2. What did you use to scoop the ice cream?   fork ☐   spoon ☐

Write the correct word beside each scrambled word.

scba _____	scodl _____	scael _____
scna _____	scaer _____	scafr _____
scta _____	scotu _____	scolw _____

Make sentences

Scarf
_____
_____

Scout
_____
_____

Rules
TRACE AND COLOR

Trace it:

SC SC SC SC

sc sc sc sc

score score

Colour it:

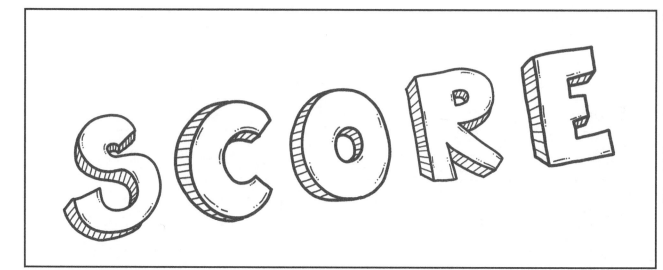

I CAN WRITE

Color Me!

score

Circle the - sc - words

scarf   span   scale

spill   scrum   phiz

scurry   droop   scowl

Trace the words

Fill in the missing letters

scar _____   scub _____

scoo _____   scru _____

scor _____   scurr _____

Read and Trace the sentence.

We have a scuba
we have a scuba

READ AGAIN

Read the story, and answer each question. highlight the answers in the story.

Brave Adventures in Nature

The nearby woods were a favorite place for Lila to explore. She decided to go for a scoop of water after spotting a small stream one day. She knelt down and saw a little rascal taking some berries from a bush close by. She turned when she heard a sudden, loud screech and noticed a bird flying overhead. She felt a little frightened, but then she recalled how brave she had been when she and her friends had gone on a scout trip. She observed the bird fly away while taking a proud stance. Lila felt good about herself and carried on with her journey, confident that she could face anything with courage and confidence.

Answer Each Question.

1 - What was Lila's favorite place to explore?

_____

2 - What did Lila spot that made her go for a scoop of water?

_____

3 - What did Lila hear that made her turn around?

_____

COLOR ME

Read and color the Letter

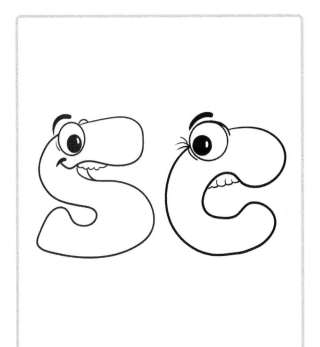

sh
I CAN READ

Read the story, and identify and underline all the - sh - words.

Shining Sheep Friendship

Sophie lived on a farm as a sheep. She was always timid and disliked being around a lot of people. She met a small girl called Sally one day while strolling around the countryside. Sally was dressed well and had a lot smaller shadow than Sophie. Sally invited Sophie to join her in her playtime. Sophie was first apprehensive, but Sally showed her a trick. She instructed Sophie to shake her wool, and Sophie did so. Sophie's wool suddenly began to gleam in the sunlight, and Sally's face lighted up with delight. Sophie and Sally were good friends after that, and Sophie recognized that sometimes you simply need to laugh.

read and write

Write all the " sh " words you can see in the story			

I CAN READ

Read the sentences and answers the questions: Put a check mark

The ship was so big

The shy girl waved hello

The sheep have soft wool

Questions

1. How big was the ship?   so big ☐   small ☐
2. Who waved hello shyly?   girl ☐   boy ☐

Write the correct word beside each scrambled word.

syh _____	shepe _____	shotr _____
shaek _____	shitr _____	shwo _____
shien _____	shaer _____	shoudl _____

Make sentences

Sheep
_____
_____

Shirt
_____
_____

Rules
TRACE AND COLOR

Trace it:

SH SH SH SH

sh sh sh sh

show   show

Colour it:

I CAN WRITE

Color Me!

Circle the - sh - words

shout	should	scale
spill	she	phiz
shirt	droop	shell

Trace the words

shirt   shirt
ship   ship
short   short

Fill in the missing letters

sho _____   shove _____
shou _____   shee _____
shrin _____ shak _____

Read and Trace the sentence.

I should go

I should go

READ AGAIN

Read the story, and answer each question. highlight the answers in the story.

Shining Sheep Friendship

Sophie lived on a farm as a sheep. She was always timid and disliked being around a lot of people. She met a small girl called Sally one day while strolling around the countryside. Sally was dressed well and had a lot smaller shadow than Sophie. Sally invited Sophie to join her in her playtime. Sophie was first apprehensive, but Sally showed her a trick. She instructed Sophie to shake her wool, and Sophie did so. Sophie's wool suddenly began to gleam in the sunlight, and Sally's face lighted up with delight. Sophie and Sally were good friends after that, and Sophie recognized that sometimes you simply need to laugh.

Answer Each Question.

1 - Where did Sophie live?

_____

2 - What did Sophie dislike?

_____

3 - What did Sally instruct Sophie to do?

_____

COLOR ME

Read and color the Letter

oi
I CAN READ

Read the story, and identify and underline all the - oi - words.

Roy's Oily Adventure

Once upon a time, there was a young child named Roy who enjoyed playing with coins. He decided to join his buddies in the garden one day to play with his new toy automobile. But, as they were playing, Roy unintentionally spilled some oil on the automobile, making it loud and difficult to drive. They tried wiping it away with foil, but it didn't work. Roy's companions have a choice: ruin their game or work together to find a solution. After some deliberation, they removed the oil with a pointed stick, and the automobile was as good as new. They were all overjoyed and even anointed the automobile with some oi-yink. They discovered this on that day.

read and write

Write all the " oi " words you can see in the story			

I CAN READ

Read the sentences and answers the questions: Put a check mark

The noisy car needed oil

It was time to toil

Soil is where plants grow

Questions

1. What did the car need?   oil ☐   wheels ☐
2. Where do plants grow?   air ☐   soil ☐

Write the correct word beside each scrambled word.

boli _____   joni _____   roli _____

coni _____   moli _____   soli _____

foli _____   oli _____   voiec _____

Make sentences

Coin
_____
_____

Voice
_____
_____

Rules
TRACE AND COLOR

Trace it:

OI OI OI OI OI

oi   oi   oi   oi

point   point

Colour it:

I CAN WRITE

Color Me!

coin

Circle the - oi - words

boil	should	foil
spill	roil	phiz
voice	droop	point

Trace the words

noisy   noisy
foil   foil
roil   roil

Fill in the missing letters

roi ____   poin ____

foi ____   recoi ____

voic ____   nois ____

Read and Trace the sentence.

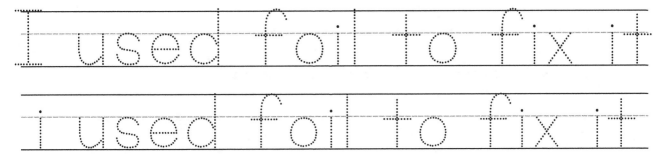

I used foil to fix it
I used foil to fix it

READ AGAIN

Read the story, and answer each question. highlight the answers in the story.

Roy's Oily Adventure

Once upon a time, there was a young child named Roy who enjoyed playing with coins. He decided to join his buddies in the garden one day to play with his new toy automobile. But, as they were playing, Roy unintentionally spilled some oil on the automobile, making it loud and difficult to drive. They tried wiping it away with foil, but it didn't work. Roy's companions have a choice: ruin their game or work together to find a solution. After some deliberation, they removed the oil with a pointed stick, and the automobile was as good as new. They were all overjoyed and even anointed the automobile with some oi-yink. They discovered this on that day.

Answer Each Question.

1 - What did Roy spill on the car?

_____

2 - What did they use to remove the oil?

_____

3 - How did Roy and his friends feel after fixing the car?

_____

COLOR ME

Read and color the Letter

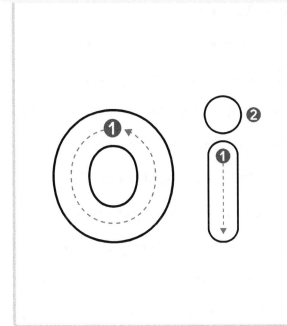
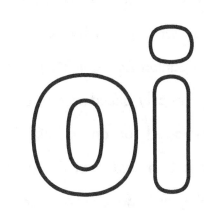

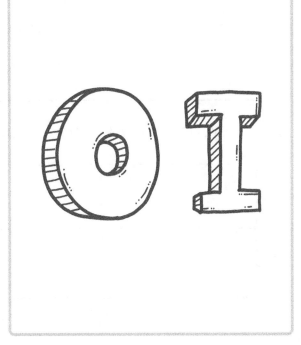

oe
I CAN READ

Read the story, and identify and underline all the - oe - words.

Joe and Zoe's Adventure

Joe was a young lad once upon a time. He stubbed his toe on a rock one day while going through the forest. He shouted out in anguish, and his companion Zoe quickly ran to his aid. When they headed back home, she promptly assisted him up and consoled him. Joe's mother noticed his damaged toe and administered some soothing ointment when they got home. She said that it was a frequent problem for youngsters who liked to play outside. Joe and Zoe went to the park the following day to play. A doe and her fawn were seen grazing nearby. They decided to approach the doe, but she grew terrified and fled, leaving the fawn behind. They came to a decision.

read and write

Write all the " oe " words you can see in the story

I CAN READ

Read the sentences and answers the questions: Put a check mark

Joey saw a doe in the meadow

Joe rode on a boat

Moe had a sore toe

Questions

1. What did Joey see in the meadow?   doe ☐   cat ☐
2. What did Joe ride on?   boat ☐   train ☐

Write the correct word beside each scrambled word.

teo _____   chleo _____   code _____

jeo _____   zeo _____   nole _____

reo _____   jole _____   deo _____

Make sentences

Toe _____
_____
_____

Hoe _____
_____
_____

Rules
TRACE AND COLOR

Trace it:

OE   OE   OE   OE

oe   oe   oe   oe

toe   toe   toe

Colour it:

 # I CAN WRITE

Color Me!

moe

Circle the - oe - words

boil	moe	foil
noel	roil	cloe
joey	droop	coed

Trace the words

Fill in the missing letters

ro ____   po ____

co ____   ho ____

to ____   mo ____

Read and Trace the sentence.

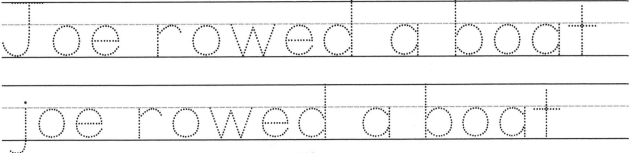

READ AGAIN

Read the story, and answer each question. highlight the answers in the story.

Joe and Zoe's Adventure

Joe was a young lad once upon a time. He stubbed his toe on a rock one day while going through the forest. He shouted out in anguish, and his companion Zoe quickly ran to his aid. When they headed back home, she promptly assisted him up and consoled him. Joe's mother noticed his damaged toe and administered some soothing ointment when they got home. She said that it was a frequent problem for youngsters who liked to play outside. Joe and Zoe went to the park the following day to play. A doe and her fawn were seen grazing nearby. They decided to approach the doe, but she grew terrified and fled, leaving the fawn behind. They came to a decision.

Answer Each Question.

1 - Who helped Joe when he hurt his toe?
_____

2 - Where did Joe and Zoe go to play?
_____

3 - What did they see at the park?
_____

COLOR ME

Read and color the Letter

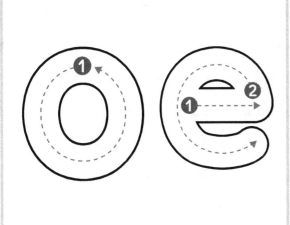

ei
I CAN READ

Read the story, and identify and underline all the - ei - words.

The Starry Reindeer

Bree was a reindeer who lived once upon a time in a lovely woodland. Bree was white with a long, flowing mane. Bree was well-known for his dexterity and ability to execute spectacular stunts with his antlers. Bree observed a weird creature that appeared like a deity one day while playing with his reindeer buddies. The monster ruled regally and emitted a radiance from its body. Bree pursued the monster to a clearing in the woodland, where he noticed a magnificent eight-pointed star hanging in the sky. Bree felt a burst of strength flood through his veins and decided to brave and attempt to touch the star. He sprang high into the air and, feigning agility.

read and write

Write all the " ei " words you can see in the story			

I CAN READ

Read the sentences and answers the questions: Put a check mark

I can count to eighty

I saw a feisty cat

The horse has shiny reins

Questions

1. What animal was feisty?   cat ☐   dog ☐
2. What animal was not tame?   bee ☐   horse ☐

Write the correct word beside each scrambled word.

eigth _____   weigth _____   veni _____

eighyt _____   freigth _____   feing _____

neighbro _____   sleigth _____   deiyt _____

Make sentences

Weight
_____
_____

Feisty
_____
_____

Rules
TRACE AND COLOR

Trace it:

E   E   E   E

ei   ei   ei   ei

eight eight eight

Colour it:

I CAN WRITE

Color Me!

Circle the - ei - words

weight	moe	foil
noel	roil	deity
reign	sleigh	coed

Trace the words

eight   eight
vein   vein
feign   feign

Fill in the missing letters

eigh____   weigh____
sleigh____ deit____
freigh____ heigh____

Read and Trace the sentence.

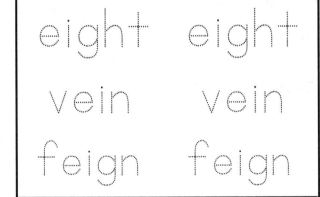

READ AGAIN

Read the story, and answer each question. highlight the answers in the story.

The Starry Reindeer

Bree was a reindeer who lived once upon a time in a lovely woodland. Bree was white with a long, flowing mane. Bree was well-known for his dexterity and ability to execute spectacular stunts with his antlers. Bree observed a weird creature that appeared like a deity one day while playing with his reindeer buddies. The monster ruled regally and emitted a radiance from its body. Bree pursued the monster to a clearing in the woodland, where he noticed a magnificent eight-pointed star hanging in the sky. Bree felt a burst of strength flood through his veins and decided to brave and attempt to touch the star. He sprang high into the air and, feigning agility.

Answer Each Question.

1 - What was Bree well-known for?

_____

2 - Where did Bree follow the creature to?

_____

3 - What did Bree attempt to touch?

_____

COLOR ME

Read and color the Letter

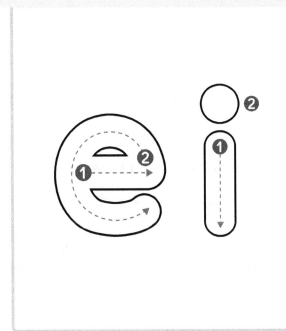
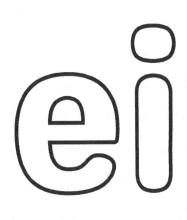

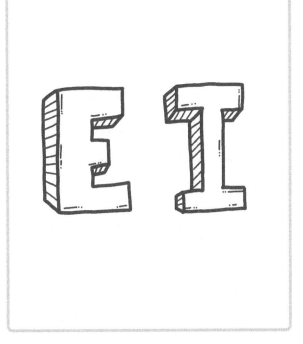

ea
I CAN READ

Read the story, and identify and underline all the - ea - words.

The Beach Feast Adventure

Once upon a time, there was a young girl named Mia who enjoyed eating fresh peaches from her garden's tree. She was so taken with them that she resolved to learn how to plant her own peach tree. Mia requested that her mother show her how to plant one, which her mother eagerly agreed to. They walked to the seashore together to choose the ideal soil for the tree. They made care to irrigate the seed every day and maintain it free of weeds once they planted it. After weeks of hard labor, a little sprout developed into a large tree. Mia was pleased to discover that her tiny seed had sprouted into a peach tree.

read and write

Write all the " ea " words you can see in the story			

I CAN READ

Read the sentences and answers the questions: Put a check mark

I like to sit on my beach chair

Mom will cook a feast

The teacher will teach us

Questions

1. What is Mom going to prepare?   feast ☐   pizza ☐
2. Who will educate us?   teacher ☐   book ☐

Write the correct word beside each scrambled word.

peahc _____   seta _____   stema _____

teahc _____   feats _____   tema _____

beahc _____   drema _____   meta _____

Make sentences

Beach
_____
_____

Dream
_____
_____

Rules
TRACE AND COLOR

Trace it:

EA EA EA EA

ea ea ea ea

bean bean bean

Colour it:

I CAN WRITE

Color Me!

clean

Circle the - ea - words

clean	feast	foil
noel	pea	team
clean	sleigh	weak

Trace the words

leap leap
seal seal
clean clean

Fill in the missing letters

clea____   mea____

lea____   stea____

pleas____ feas____

Read and Trace the sentence.

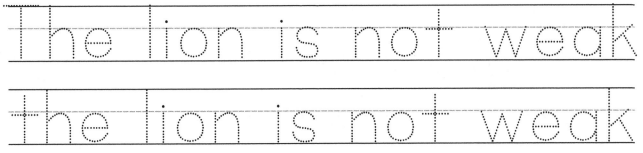

READ AGAIN

Read the story, and answer each question. highlight the answers in the story.

The Beach Feast Adventure

Once upon a time, there was a young girl named Mia who enjoyed eating fresh peaches from her garden's tree. She was so taken with them that she resolved to learn how to plant her own peach tree. Mia requested that her mother show her how to plant one, which her mother eagerly agreed to. They walked to the seashore together to choose the ideal soil for the tree. They made care to irrigate the seed every day and maintain it free of weeds once they planted it. After weeks of hard labor, a little sprout developed into a large tree. Mia was pleased to discover that her tiny seed had sprouted into a peach tree.

Answer Each Question.

1 - Who enjoyed eating fresh peaches?
_____

2 - What did Mia resolve to do?
_____

3 - Where did they go to choose soil?
_____

COLOR ME

Read and color the Letter

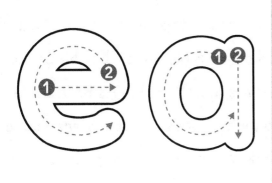

au
I CAN READ

Read the story, and identify and underline all the - au - words.

The Beach Feast Adventure

Pauls the astronaut was prepared to launch his spacecraft to explore the galaxy one sunny day. He accidentally set fire to his outfit while fuelling the spaceship! He swiftly extinguished the flames, although it was his fault for not being more cautious. Pauls moved on with his quest, but he couldn't shake the sensation that the error was haunting him. As he traveled through the universe, he came to a planet whose people were sauce specialists. They taught him how to cook a fantastic sausage meal that he could take home with him. The flavor impressed August, prompting him to commend the outstanding cooks. When Pauls returned to Earth, he introduced his new dish, which quickly became a fan favorite.

read and write

Write all the " au " words you can see in the story

I CAN READ

Read the sentences and answers the questions: Put a check mark

I caught a big fish

The car's fault was fixed

I like sauce on pasta

Questions

1. What did you catch?   big fish ☐   small fish ☐
2. What do you like sauce on?   pasta ☐   pizza ☐

Write the correct word beside each scrambled word.

fautl _____   sauec _____   pausl _____

launhc _____   caues _____   dautn _____

hautn _____   vautl _____   sautl _____

Make sentences

Launch
_____
_____

August
_____
_____

Rules
TRACE AND COLOR

Trace it:

AU AU AU AU

au au au au

haunt haunt

Colour it:

I CAN WRITE

Color Me!

launch

Circle the - au - words

launch   feast   haunt

vault   pea   daunt

clean   author   weak

Trace the words

sauce sauce
cause cause
faulty faulty

Fill in the missing letters

traum_____   paul_____

saun_____   sauc_____

claus_____   haun_____

Read and Trace the sentence.

Pauls likes to play

pauls likes to play

READ AGAIN

Read the story, and answer each question. highlight the answers in the story.

The Beach Feast Adventure

Pauls the astronaut was prepared to launch his spacecraft to explore the galaxy one sunny day. He accidentally set fire to his outfit while fuelling the spaceship! He swiftly extinguished the flames, although it was his fault for not being more cautious. Pauls moved on with his quest, but he couldn't shake the sensation that the error was haunting him. As he traveled through the universe, he came to a planet whose people were sauce specialists. They taught him how to cook a fantastic sausage meal that he could take home with him. The flavor impressed August, prompting him to commend the outstanding cooks. When Pauls returned to Earth, he introduced his new dish, which quickly became a fan favorite.

Answer Each Question.

1 - What did Pauls prepare to launch?

_____

2 - What happened while he was fuelling the spaceship?

_____

3 - Whose fault was it?

_____

COLOR ME

Read and color the Letter

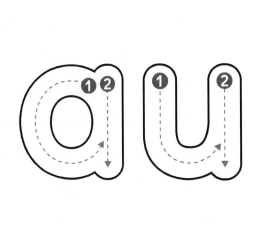

aw
I CAN READ

Read the story, and identify and underline all the - aw - words.

Fawn and Raw

One sunny day, a little fawn was playing in a field. Suddenly, he heard a loud noise. It was a hawk, circling above him. The fawn was scared and wanted to run away, but he had hurt his paw earlier and couldn't move quickly. Just then, a kind man saw the fawn's distress and rushed over to help. He scooped up the fawn and brought him to his home. The man had a big, friendly dog named Raw who became the fawn's new friend. They played together in the lawn and had a great time. Later that day, the man took out a saw and built a new shelter for the fawn. It was cozy and warm, with straw bedding and plenty of space. The fawn was very happy in his new home, with his new friend Raw by his side.

read and write

Write all the " aw " words you can see in the story

I CAN READ

Read the sentences and answers the questions: Put a check mark

The cat has sharp claws

The lawn needs watering

I bought a new straw hat

Questions

1. What does the cat have? claws ☐   toy ☐
2. What needs watering? lawn ☐   tree ☐

Write the correct word beside each scrambled word.

lwa _____	strwa _____	flwa _____
pwa _____	clwa _____	bralw _____
swa _____	drwa _____	crwa _____

Make sentences

Draw _____
_____

Flaw _____
_____

Rules
TRACE AND COLOR

Trace it:

A W   A W   A W

aw   aw   aw   aw

draw   draw

Colour it:

I CAN WRITE

Color Me!

fawn

Circle the - aw - words

jaw	claw	haunt
vault	draw	daunt
clean	lawn	weak

Trace the words

slaw   slaw
craw   craw
pawn   pawn

Fill in the missing letters

dra ——   paw ——
stra ——   yaw ——
fla ——   braw ——

Read and Trace the sentence.

I saw a hawk fly
i saw a hawk fly

READ AGAIN

Read the story, and answer each question. highlight the answers in the story.

Fawn and Raw

One sunny day, a little fawn was playing in a field. Suddenly, he heard a loud noise. It was a hawk, circling above him. The fawn was scared and wanted to run away, but he had hurt his paw earlier and couldn't move quickly. Just then, a kind man saw the fawn's distress and rushed over to help. He scooped up the fawn and brought him to his home. The man had a big, friendly dog named Raw who became the fawn's new friend. They played together in the lawn and had a great time. Later that day, the man took out a saw and built a new shelter for the fawn. It was cozy and warm, with straw bedding and plenty of space. The fawn was very happy in his new home, with his new friend Raw by his side.

Answer Each Question.

1 - Where was the fawn playing?
_____

2 - What scared the fawn?
_____

3 - Who helped the fawn?
_____

COLOR ME

Read and color the Letter

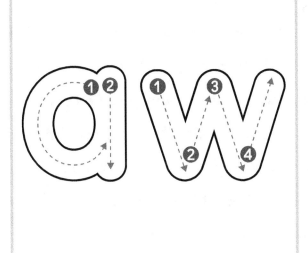

ew
I CAN READ

Read the story, and identify and underline all the - ew - words.

Drew's Delicious Stew

One sunny day, a farmer named Drew was making a big stew for his crew. He added new vegetables and herbs he had grown on his farm. While he was cooking, his son Hugh came over to help. Hugh noticed that the pot was too small for the stew, so he went to get a new one. As he was walking back, he slipped on some dew and dropped the new pot. Drew wasn't mad and he told Hugh that it was okay. They used a few towels to clean up the mess and continued cooking. When the stew was done, Drew served it in new bowls and everyone sat down to eat. It was so delicious that they all said "yum" with every chew.

read and write

Write all the " ew " words you can see in the story

I CAN READ

Read the sentences and answers the questions: Put a check mark

The morning dew was sparkling

My mom bought me a new toy

I saw a few birds in the park

Questions

1. What did your mom buy for you?   toy ☐   bike ☐
2. What did you see in the park?   birds ☐   trees ☐

Write the correct word beside each scrambled word.

chwe ____	stwe ____	crwe ____
dwe ____	pwe ____	jwe ____
nwe ____	fwe ____	blwe ____

Make sentences

Knew
_____
_____

New
_____
_____

Rules
TRACE AND COLOR

Trace it:

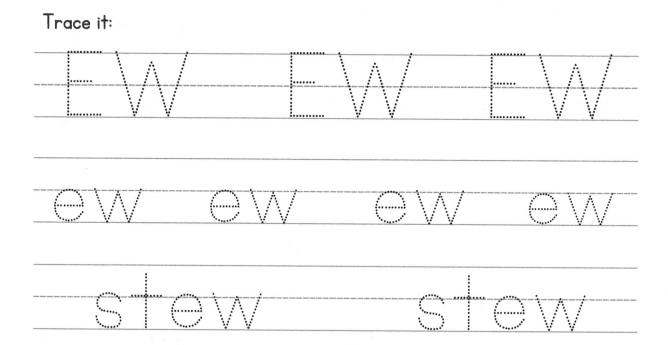

Colour it:

I CAN WRITE

Color Me!

crew

Circle the - ew - words

jaw	pew	sew
vault	drew	daunt
grew	lawn	knew

Trace the words

Fill in the missing letters

gre ____   ste ____

kne ____   de ____

cre ____   che ____

Read and Trace the sentence.

The morning dew

the morning dew

READ AGAIN

Read the story, and answer each question. highlight the answers in the story.

Drew's Delicious Stew

One sunny day, a farmer named Drew was making a big stew for his crew. He added new vegetables and herbs he had grown on his farm. While he was cooking, his son Hugh came over to help. Hugh noticed that the pot was too small for the stew, so he went to get a new one. As he was walking back, he slipped on some dew and dropped the new pot. Drew wasn't mad and he told Hugh that it was okay. They used a few towels to clean up the mess and continued cooking. When the stew was done, Drew served it in new bowls and everyone sat down to eat. It was so delicious that they all said "yum" with every chew.

Answer Each Question.

1 - Who was making a big stew for his crew?

_____

2 - What did Hugh notice about the pot while his dad was cooking?

_____

3 - Was Drew mad at Hugh for dropping the pot?

_____

COLOR ME

Read and color the Letter

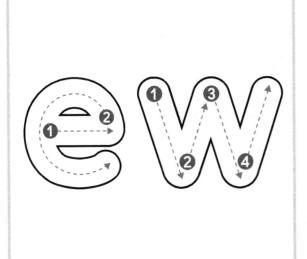

THANK YOU

Thank you for choosing this decodable book for your child in kindergarten. I appreciate your trust in my work and I hope this book will prove to be a valuable tool in your child's reading journey.

As a writer, my goal has always been to create resources that promote reading and make it an enjoyable experience for young readers. This book is designed to help struggling readers improve their decoding skills and gain confidence in their reading abilities.

I have taken a structured approach in this book, teaching children the sounds that letters make in a specific order. I have also included activities in each passage that are designed to reinforce phonemic awareness and promote skill development. My hope is that with the help of this book, your child will build a solid foundation in reading and become a confident and proficient reader in no time.

Once again, thank you for choosing this book. I would love to hear your feedback on this book and how it has helped your child. Your opinion matters to me and it will assist me in creating more valuable resources for young readers in the future.

Thank you for your support and happy reading!

Best regards,

[Jed Dolton]